# WAY TO GO!

## Finding Your Way
### with a Compass

Written by Sharon Sharth
Illustrated by David Wenzel

Reader's Digest Children's Books™
Pleasantville, New York • Montréal, Québec

READER'S DIGEST CHILDREN'S BOOKS
Reader's Digest Road
Pleasantville, NY 10570-7000

The topographical map on page 37 is reprinted courtesy of the United States Geological Survey.

Manufactured in China.
10 9 8 7 6 5 4 3 2

Library of Congress Cataloging-in-Publication Data

Sharth, Sharon.
   Way to go! : finding your way with a compass / written by Sharon Sharth ; illustrated by David Wenzel.
         p. cm. — (Reader's Digest explorer guides)
   Includes index.
   ISBN 1-57584-966-6 (paperback)
   1. Orienteering—Juvenile literature. 2. Nature study—Activity programs—Juvenile literature. [1. Compass. 2. Orienteering. 3. Nature study.] I. Wenzel, David, 1950- ill. II. Title. III. Series.

   GV200.4 .S53 2000                    796.58—dc21                    00-028614

# Contents

# Let's Go for a Hike!

Exploring nature is fun. If you go hiking in the woods, you might see a deer and her fawns picking their way through the trees. Walking through a meadow, you may spot a Red-tailed Hawk being badgered by crows. In autumn, you can enjoy the colorful leaves while songbirds migrate overhead. In winter, you might see the tracks of small animals in the snow.

What isn't fun? Losing your way. That can be scary! But you don't have to take a chance on getting lost. There are plenty of ways to figure out where you are and where you're going. Knowing how to navigate, or find your way, will give you confidence while you explore. Your compass can help to guide you. So can the sun and the stars. Read on and discover how you can stay found.

# Before You Start Out

The first rule is to be prepared. Plan your route. Even though you may not be going far, know where you're headed. Make sure someone knows where you're going and how long you expect to be gone. Don't go exploring alone. Take a grown-up and a friend or two along.

Pay attention to the weather. Is it changing? How much sunlight is left? You'll want to be back at camp or home by dark. Wear a watch.

Always carry water. If you're going to be gone for a while, put some snacks in your backpack.

> **DON'T FORGET**
> During the winter months, the days are shorter and the sun will set earlier.

Dress for the season. If it's winter, dress warmly. If it's warm out, take along a sweater or a light jacket. You might need it if the temperature changes—especially in the spring or fall. If it's summer, use sunscreen and insect repellent. Wear sturdy shoes or hiking boots.

In this book, you'll learn how to use a compass and a map. Always travel with them! Every time you change direction, check your compass. It will keep you from going too far off course. Watch for landmarks, or objects that stand out. They'll guide you on your journey and help you find your way home.

Clean up after yourself. Take your trash home with you. Leave nature the way you found it. The wild animals and other explorers will thank you!

cap

compass

water bottle

watch

flashlight

map

backpack

sturdy shoes

# What to Do if You Get Lost

If you do happen to get lost, don't panic. Hug a tree! Make that tree your home base. It will give you shelter. Now, sit down. Take a drink of water. Eat a snack. Breathe slowly— in and out, in and out. When you're calm, check your map and compass. Get up and walk around your tree in a circle, slowly going farther and farther away. Look for landmarks you recognize. Maybe you passed a tree that was scorched by lightning. Can you see it? Did you cross a stream? Listen for the sound of flowing water. Still lost? Go back to your tree. Relax. Your companions will be looking for you. If they can't find you, they will send searchers, who will.

> **LIGHTNING ALERT**
> The only time you should not hug a tree is during a thunderstorm. Stay away from all high points and get low to the ground. You can still find shelter under a bush or even a large rock.

## TRAIL MIX

Hansel and Gretel scattered bread crumbs along their trail through the woods. They thought they'd be able to follow the crumbs back home, but birds and other forest animals ate them. Marking your trail is a good idea, but what would work better than bread crumbs?

## THE HOME BASE SYSTEM

The Australian Aborigines use this method to explore their world. These wandering tribal people become familiar with an area by taking short trips away from camp. Each day they walk farther away, memorizing landmarks as they go.

9

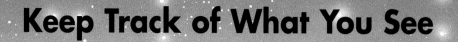

Use a notebook or journal to help you keep track of where you go and what you see. Watch for animals. Maybe you'll see a turtle basking on a rock or a fox peeking through the underbrush. Listen. What noises do animals make? Could that tapping be a woodpecker looking for food in a tree? Write down what you hear. Look for animal tracks and droppings.

What smells do you notice? Any skunks on your route? Is the ocean nearby? Can you smell it? Wind gusting toward shore smells different than wildflowers. Which way is the wind blowing? Watch how trees and other plants bend and sway. Instead of picking flowers, draw them.

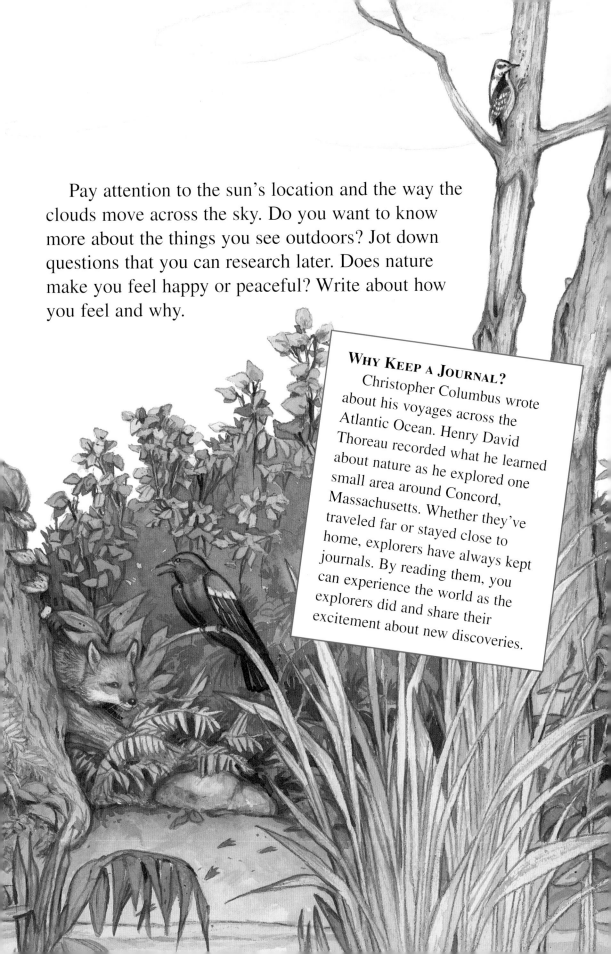

Pay attention to the sun's location and the way the clouds move across the sky. Do you want to know more about the things you see outdoors? Jot down questions that you can research later. Does nature make you feel happy or peaceful? Write about how you feel and why.

### WHY KEEP A JOURNAL?

Christopher Columbus wrote about his voyages across the Atlantic Ocean. Henry David Thoreau recorded what he learned about nature as he explored one small area around Concord, Massachusetts. Whether they've traveled far or stayed close to home, explorers have always kept journals. By reading them, you can experience the world as the explorers did and share their excitement about new discoveries.

# Navigating by the Sun and Stars

Explorers have used the sun and the stars to help them find their way for hundreds and hundreds of years. This is called celestial navigation. In AD 800, the Vikings used a bearing dial to cross the Atlantic Ocean. Sailors like Christopher Columbus used tools such as the astrolabe and the quadrant to stay on course. The cross-staff was invented in the early 1500s, and sextants in the 1700s. All these tools measured the height, or altitude, of the sun or other stars above the horizon. And once they knew that, sailors could figure out the latitude of their ship, or how far north or south they were.

The astrolabe was invented more than 2,000 years ago.

The cross-staff took the movement of the ship into account. This made it more exact than earlier tools.

To use the quadrant, the sailor aimed one straight edge at a star. Where the weight crossed the scale on the curved edge gave him the altitude.

The sextant measured altitude with a telescope, two mirrors, and a scale.

# Navigating by Day

The sun rises in the east in the morning. It sets in the west. That's because Earth turns from west to east. Which way is east at your house? Does the sun stream through your bedroom windows before school and wake you up? Those windows might be facing east. Or is it so dark in your room that you want to keep sleeping? Your room might be on the west side of the house. You can use the sun to figure out which way is which.

## How to Tell Direction by Using the Sun

### What You'll Need

A sunny day

Compass

### What to Do

1. Get up early and go outside.
2. Stand with your right arm pointing toward the rising sun. That's east.
3. Point your left arm the opposite way, where the sun will set. That's west.
4. Look straight ahead. You're facing north!
5. Now, check your compass. The part of the needle marked **N** should be pointing in the same direction you're facing, or north.
6. Turn all the way around (180 degrees) so that you're facing in the opposite direction.
7. Point toward the sunrise with your left hand. That's east.
8. Point toward where the sun will set with your right hand. That's west.
9. Now you're facing south.
10. Check your compass. The part of the needle marked **S** should be pointing the same way you're facing, or south.

# Time Will Tell

Standard time is based on where the sun is in the sky. Even when we turn our clocks ahead one hour for daylight saving time, the sun is still on standard time. So if it's daylight saving time where you live, turn your watch back one hour before you try the next two ways to find direction.

## How to Find South by Using a Watch

**What You'll Need**

A sunny day

Watch (use one that has hands—a digital watch won't work!)

Compass

**What to Do**

1. Hold the watch flat in the palm of your hand.
2. Point the hour hand (the little one) in the direction of the sun.
3. Halfway between the 12 and the hour hand is south.
4. Now check your compass. The part of the needle marked **S** should be pointing in the same direction—south.

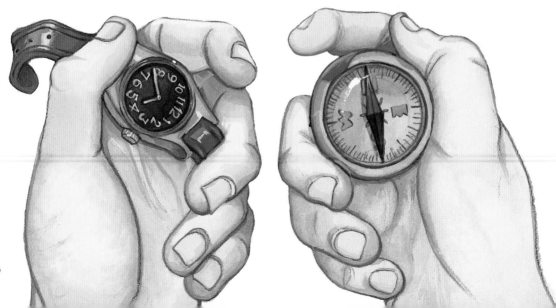

## How to Find North by Using a Shadow Stick

### What You'll Need

A sunny day

Straight stick

String (as long as the stick) with a nail tied at one end

2 rocks

Compass

---

### What to Do

1. Push one end of the stick into a patch of dirt. Make sure the stick is standing straight up.

2. Tie the free end of the string to the bottom of the stick.

3. Pull the string out from the stick until it's straight. Drag the nail across the ground to make a circle around the stick.

4. At about 10 AM, place a rock at the tip of the stick's shadow.

5. At 2 PM, mark the tip of the stick's shadow with the other rock.

6. Stand behind the stick, facing halfway between the two rocks. You're facing north! What time would this be on your "sun clock"?

7. Check your compass. Does the part of the needle marked **N** point the same way?

 SHRINKING SHADOW

The shadow of the stick will be shortest at noon when the sun is at its highest point in the sky.

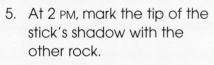

Ursa Major
(the Great Bear)

The Big
Dipper is part
of Ursa Major

Orion
(the Hunter)

# Navigating by Night

The stars rise in the east and set in the west, just like our brightest star, the sun. The stars move together in the same direction across the sky. The people of ancient civilizations figured out how to follow the stars to get where they were going. You can learn to read the stars, too.

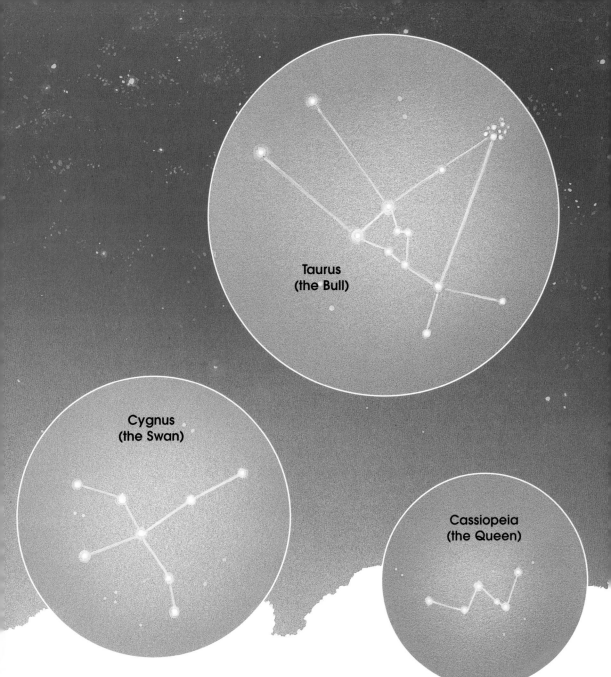

Taurus
(the Bull)

Cygnus
(the Swan)

Cassiopeia
(the Queen)

## Also known as…

Did you know that the same constellations, or star groups that form a pattern, are seen in many parts of the world? The ancient Greeks named one constellation Orion, the hunter. In China, the same constellation was called Tsan, the warrior. In Egypt, it was known as Osiris, the god of the underworld.

# As the World Turns

Everyone says that the sun and the other stars rise and set, but don't forget that it's really Earth that's turning, not the sky! Earth spins on its axis, making one complete rotation every day.

## How to Observe the Night Sky

### What You'll Need

- A starry night
- Journal

> This activity works best if you face east or south.

### What to Do

1. Make sure all outside lights are turned off before you go outside. The stars will be much easier to see. It helps if you're away from the bright lights of a city.

2. Look up at the sky and choose a group of stars that you can easily identify. (Are there three stars in a straight line? Does a group of stars appear to make a **W**?)

3. Find a fixed object, or landmark, that appears to be near your group of stars. A tree branch, a chimney, or the corner of a roof makes a good landmark.

4. Stand in the same spot for a few minutes three different times during the night. Find your landmark and look for your group of stars. Did they stay in the same place, or did they move away from your landmark? Did the stars stay in the same group?

5. Do this for a week, and record your observations every night.

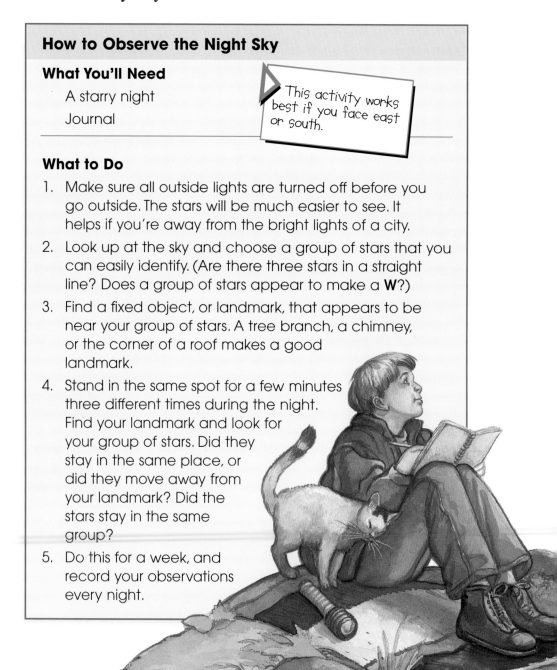

## The Center of the Universe?

Our ancestors thought that the sun, the planets, and the stars revolved around Earth. In the 1500s, a man named Copernicus wrote that the sun was at the center of the universe. In 1609, Galileo was the first person to look at the sky through a telescope. He agreed with Copernicus. But it took another 100 years for most people to believe it. And it was only 80 years ago that astronomers showed that the sun wasn't the center of the universe, either!

**WANDERING STARS**
Did you know that the planets were called "wandering stars" by early astronomers? Why? Because the planets appear to move forward in relation to the stars, then stop and loop back in the opposite direction.

# Look for the North Star

There is one star that doesn't move. It's Polaris, or the North Star. Earth's axis points toward the North Star. Find it and you'll know where north is. You can locate the North Star by finding the Big Dipper.

## How to Find the North Star

### What You'll Need

A starry night

### What to Do

1. Look up at the sky. Find the constellation that looks like a huge pot with a handle. That's the Big Dipper.

2. Find the two bright stars on the side of the pot opposite the handle.

3. Imagine a line that starts with the star at the bottom of the pot and runs through the star at the top.

4. Keep following the line and you'll find the North Star. It's at the end of the handle of the Little Dipper.

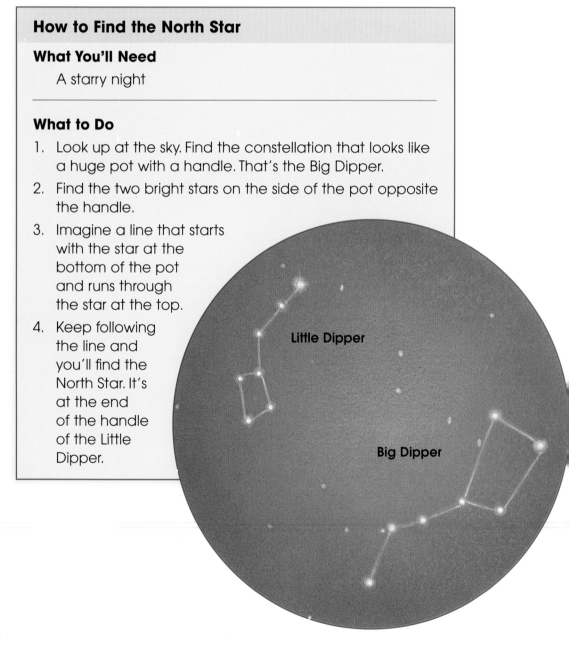

Little Dipper

Big Dipper

## Plan Ahead

You know how to find north on a starry night or a sunny day. But what if you want to know where north is when the stars are no longer twinkling and clouds hide the sun? Try this!

### How to Make a Direction Finder

**What You'll Need**

A starry night
2 sticks (one longer, one shorter)

**What to Do**

1. Find the North Star.
2. Push the longer stick into the ground so that it stands straight up.
3. Keep looking at the North Star. Now, back up a few feet from the first stick and push the shorter stick into the ground so that it's standing straight up.
4. In the morning, stand behind the short stick and face in the direction of the longer stick. You are looking north! Now you have a direction finder that will work even when it's cloudy.

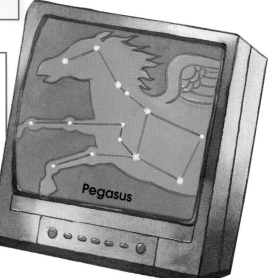

Pegasus

THAT'S ENTERTAINMENT!

In ancient times, people watched the stars the way we watch television today. They named the constellations after gods and heroes, and told stories about their adventures. Can you come up with some exciting adventures by looking up at the night sky?

Orion

# Navigating with a Compass

A compass is a tool that helps you to figure out which way you're going. Hold your compass flat and steady or place it on the ground. Its needle looks pretty wobbly, but when it is still, the needle will always point toward Earth's magnetic north. Why?

Earth is a giant magnet! The outer core of Earth is mostly made of hot, liquid iron. Scientists think that as Earth rotates, the liquid moves in spiral currents. These currents create electricity, which produces a magnetic field. Just like any other magnet's, the force of Earth's magnetic field moves from pole to pole. The magnetized needle in your compass is drawn to Earth's magnetic poles.

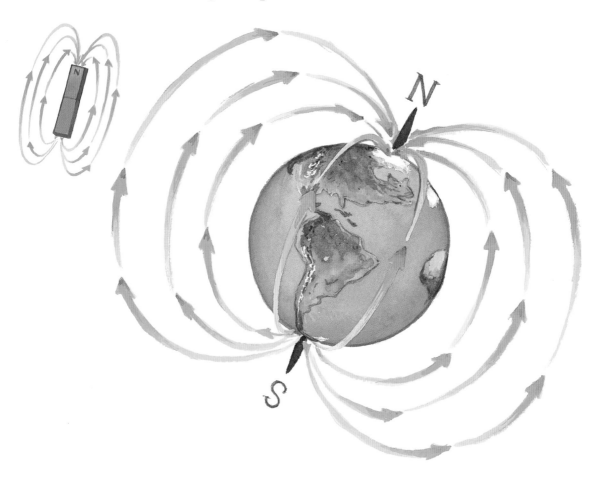

### TRADING PLACES

Some scientists believe that every so often, Earth's magnetic poles trade places. Why? Because they've found iron-containing rocks on the ocean floor that have reversed magnetic poles. Based on how old the rocks are, scientists think Earth's magnetic poles switch places about every 500,000 years!

# Opposites Attract

The Chinese invented the compass more than 2,000 years ago. Instead of a needle, the first compass had a spoon. And instead of pointing north, the handle pointed south!

Have you heard the expression "opposites attract"? That's true for magnets. The Chinese were probably the first to discover that the mineral magnetite could attract (pull toward) and repel (push away from) certain metals. Like Earth, every magnet has a north pole and a south pole. Opposite poles attract and like poles repel. That means you can't get two north poles or two south poles to come together. And you can't keep a north pole and south pole apart! Let's see how it works.

## How Magnets Work

### What You'll Need

    2 bar magnets
    String
    A friend
    Journal

### What to Do

1. Tie a piece of string around the middle of one magnet.

2. Hold the end of the string so the magnet is suspended in the air. When the magnet stops swinging, one end will point north, just like the needle of a compass.

3. Have your friend hold the other magnet and move toward you. What happens?

4. Have your friend turn the magnet around and move toward you again. What happens?

5. Write your conclusions in your journal.

### It's Magic!

Drop a paper clip into a glass of water. Ask a friend to remove the clip without spilling the water or putting anything into the glass. When your friend gives up, use a magnet to pull the paper clip up and out along the side of the glass.

# Make Your Own Compass

How a compass works is pretty amazing. But you might be surprised to know that it's amazingly easy to make a compass. And your homemade compass will point you in the right direction as surely as the compass that came with this book!

## How to Make a Compass

### What You'll Need

Sewing needle
Magnet
Small nail
Waterproof marker
Bowl with wide rim
Water
Small leaf

### What to Do

1. Rub the needle with the magnet. Be careful not to prick your finger! Make sure you rub only toward the point of the needle, and always rub in the same direction. Do this 20 or 30 times.

2. The magnet makes the needle magnetic. To test it, try picking up the nail with your needle. If it doesn't work, repeat step 1.

3. Use the marker to write the letter **N** on the rim of the bowl. Directly across from **N**, write the letter **S**. Turn the bowl so that you are looking at the **N**. Write the letter **E** on the right side of the bowl, halfway between **N** and **S**. Write the letter **W** on the left side across from the **E**.

4. Fill the bowl halfway with water.

5. Drop the leaf into the bowl so that it floats on top of the water.

6. Place your needle gently on top of the leaf.

7. When the leaf stops moving, the needle will point north. Turn your bowl until the needle points toward the **N** you wrote. You've made a compass!

## A Compass Plant

Have you ever heard of the compass plant? The edges of its large lower leaves point north and south! Found in the prairies of the American Midwest, the compass plant is related to the common sunflower and grows about 8 feet (2.4 m) high. Sometimes called pilot weed, the compass plant helped to guide many westward-bound pioneers.

# Using Your Compass

When you know how to find north, you can find south, east, and west. These four directions are called cardinal points. Look at your compass. 0, or 360, degrees marks north. Moving clockwise, or toward your right hand, east is at 90 degrees. South is directly opposite of north, at 180 degrees. West is toward your left hand at 270 degrees. See if you can figure out how many degrees northeast is from north. How about southwest?

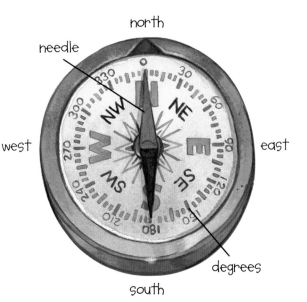

needle

north

west

east

degrees

south

## WHICH WAY TO THE NORTH POLE?

Magnetic north is different from Earth's geographical north, which is found at the very top of Earth's axis. The needle of the magnetic compass points in the direction of magnetic north—a little bit east or west of true north, depending on where you are in the world. Follow the North Star, and you're heading toward true north.

The gyrocompass points to true north and is not affected by Earth's magnetism. Once its direction is set, its spinning wheels, or rotors, resist any change in direction.

## Get Your Bearings

### What You'll Need

Compass

1 index card marked with a red **X**

10 index cards, labeled 1 to 10

Journal

A friend

> ### DON'T FORGET
> When you take readings, make sure your compass is far away from iron and steel. If you're too close, the compass needle will be attracted to those metals, and your readings will be off.

---

### What to Do

1. Put the index card marked with the red **X** on the ground and place your compass on it. You will take all your compass readings from this spot.

2. Place the 10 index cards in different places around the backyard. Make sure you can see them from the compass.

3. Once the compass needle is still, make sure it is pointing to the **N**. Don't move the compass.

4. Now, take a bearing, or compass reading. First, look at the index card labeled 1. Then use your imagination to draw an invisible line from the card to the compass. Where does the line meet the compass? Write the number of degrees in your journal.

5. Repeat step 4 for each index card.

6. Now ask your friend to take a bearing on the cards. Do your compass readings match?

# Navigating with a Map

A map shows a picture of Earth as if you were looking down from the sky. In fact, today, most maps are made from pictures taken by satellites. A map may show a park, a city, a country, a continent, or the whole Earth.

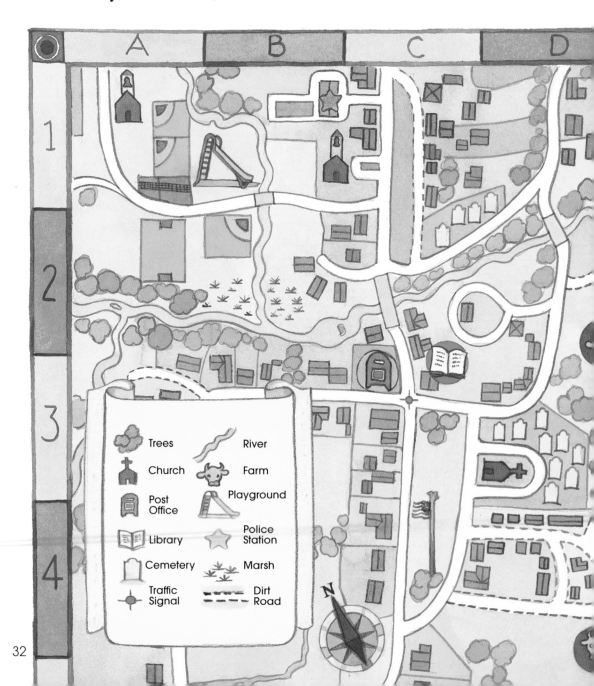

Trees

Church

Post Office

Library

Cemetery

Traffic Signal

River

Farm

Playground

Police Station

Marsh

Dirt Road

There are many different kinds of maps. Physical maps highlight features of nature, such as mountains, rivers, and lakes. Political maps show the borders of counties, states, and countries. Road maps show you what roads you can take to get from one place to another.

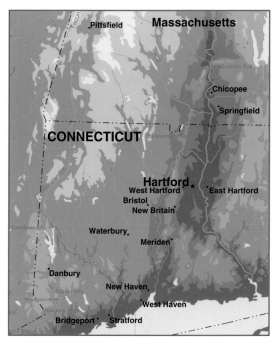

**Physical Map**

**Political Map**

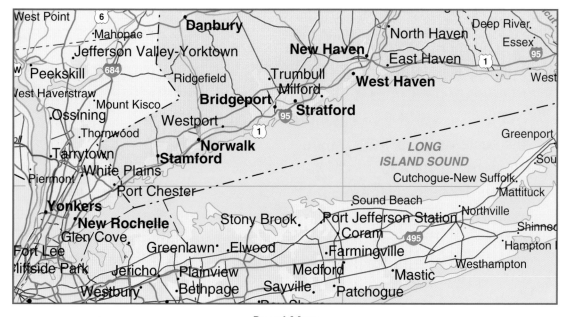

**Road Map**

# How to Read a Map

Maps are much smaller than anything they show. Because of this, mapmakers use symbols, or markings, to stand for real things. A squiggly blue line may stand for a river. A green blotch may picture a park. Two red lines drawn close together may show the route of an interstate highway. Other symbols might be the silhouette of an airplane for an airport or a square with a cross on top for a church. Look for the "key" or "legend" on your map to find out what the symbols stand for.

Key to Map Symbols

LEGEND

HIGHWAY

CAMPGROUND

RIVER

AIRPORT

MARSH

CAPITAL

STATE PARK

The map's scale tells you how far it is from one place to another—on your map and in the real world. For example, the scale on your map may show that 1 inch (2.5 cm) equals 10 miles (16 km). If your map shows that your town is 3 inches (7.6 cm) from your friend's town, that means you live 30 miles (about 48 km) apart.

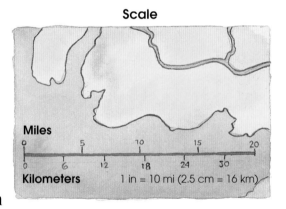

Scale

Miles

Kilometers    1 in = 10 mi (2.5 cm = 16 km)

Most of the time, your map will be drawn so that north is at the top. While some maps mark only north, many have a compass symbol that shows all the cardinal points (north, south, east, and west). The compass rose shows 32 points of direction! It has been used on maps since the 1300s. When sailors first went to sea, they had to learn the names of all 32 points. This was called "boxing the compass."

## Orienting Your Map

Look around you. Do you see a river on your left and a road on your right? Is there a town or mountain in front of you? Now look at the symbols on the map that stand for these landmarks. Turn the map so that the symbols match the real landmarks. Line your compass up with the magnetic north arrow on the map. Which direction are you facing in? Where is the river? Where are the other landmarks you can see? Knowing where you are will help you get to where you want to go.

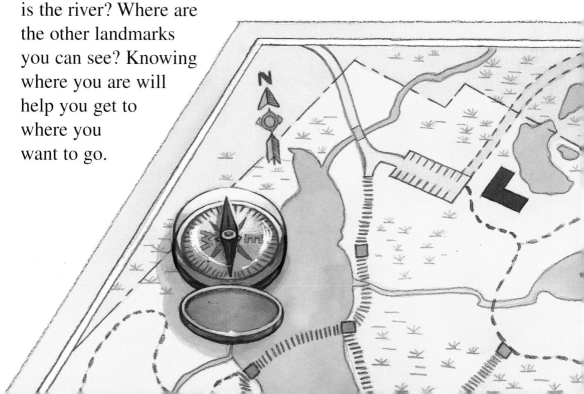

# Make Your Own Map

Now that you know how to read a map, try making one of your own.

## Drawing a Map

### What You'll Need

A friend
Paper
2 pencils
2 rulers
Compass
Red marker

### What to Do

1. Choose an outdoor area, like your backyard or a nearby park or playground, to map.

2. Now you and your friend each use a ruler to draw a map of the area. Put in things like bushes, trees, sidewalks, swing sets—as many things as you can. Use the compass to figure out which way is north.

3. Next, pick a spot in the area that will be your destination. Put a red **X** on the map to show where it is. Have your friend do the same.

4. Switch maps with your friend. Have your friend use your map to find the place you marked with the red **X**.

5. Now you do the same with your friend's map.

## Staying on Top of Things

A topographical map is a good map to have with you on a hike. It shows you where the trails are and where they lead. It shows landmarks so you can check to make sure you're in the right place. It tells you how high the land is, and what kind of land you'll be walking over. Each wavy line (called a "contour" line) connects ground that is on the same level. If you followed one line wherever it went, you would not go up or down—even if you were walking around a mountain. When the wavy lines are close together, the land is steep. When the lines are far apart, the land is more even.

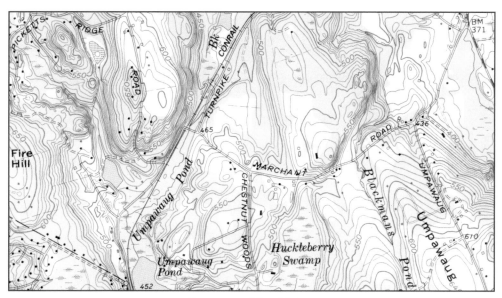

**Topographical Map**

# Navigating with GPS

Did you know that travelers still use the sky to find their way? GPS, or Global Positioning System, is a new navigating tool. It can be used at any time of the day in any kind of weather. And it can tell you exactly where you are. Here's how it works.

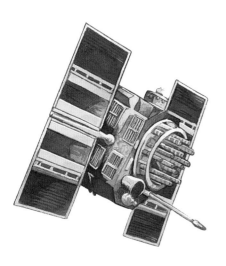

Twenty-four satellites were put into six different orbits more than 11,000 miles (17,700 km) high. There are four satellites in each orbit, and each satellite takes 12 hours to make one trip around Earth. This means that at least six of the satellites can "see" the same spot on Earth at the same time. The satellites send out position and time signals. If you have a receiver, you can pick up the signals to find out where you are.

Airplane pilots use GPS. So do mapmakers and explorers. People who study wildlife use GPS to track animals. Police and firefighters use GPS to help save lives. Your parents can buy a car with a GPS receiver. And you can get a handheld GPS receiver to take with you on a hike.

# Navigating Is for the Birds

Do you ever wonder how animals find their way from place to place? When they migrate, some animals travel thousands of miles. Arctic Terns fly from the North Pole to the South Pole—and back again. That's 22,000 miles (135,405 km) every year! Monarch butterflies fly from Canada to Mexico and back. Caribou, sea turtles, salmon, eels, and whales migrate, too. How do they keep from getting lost?

## WHICH WAY DO WE GO?

A young bird is migrating for the first time. How does it know where to go? Almost as soon as they hatch, some birds will follow their parent. This is called imprinting. Baby birds have imprinted on people, too. In one project, several young Sandhill Cranes and Whooping Cranes imprinted on a naturalist. When the birds were old enough to migrate, he took off in an ultralight airplane. The young birds followed the plane from Idaho to New Mexico. There, they joined the wild cranes at their wintering grounds.

Just like people, animals use landmarks to figure out where they are. Some use their sense of smell. Birds follow the wind and fishes follow water currents. Animals also use celestial navigation. Scientists have shown that birds can tell direction by the sun. Birds

### A BUILT-IN COMPASS?

Some animals use Earth's magnetic field to navigate. How? They have small amounts of magnetite in their bodies. This magnetic mineral may act as a built-in compass. Magnetite has been found in bacteria, birds, fishes, and bees. It's even been found in people!

that fly at night use the stars. Some sand fleas, beetles, and fishes use the sun and stars to find their way, too.

# There's No Place Like Home!

Some birds can find their way home—even when they've been carried thousands of miles away. A Manx Shearwater was taken from an island near Wales. It was let go in Massachusetts. The bird flew across the Atlantic Ocean and was back home in 12½ days. An albatross flew from Washington to its home on Midway Island in the Pacific Ocean. It made the trip of about 3,200 miles (5,150 km) in just over ten days.

## Swimming in Circles

Loggerhead sea turtles are born on the beaches of Florida. When they migrate, they follow the currents of the North Atlantic Ocean. They swim north to South Carolina, east to Portugal, south to the Equator, and west to the Caribbean. They do this for about 15 years. Then each turtle returns to the same beach where it was born to lay its eggs!

## King of the Road

Millions of monarch butterflies fly south for the winter. The monarchs that live east of the Rocky Mountains travel the farthest. They start out in Canada or the northern United States and fly all the way to Mexico. That's up to 3,000 miles (4,828 km) or more! The butterflies always return to the same places their parents used the year before. Sometimes they even cluster in the same trees. How do they do it? No one knows.

### DISAPPEARING ACT

Long ago, no one knew where birds went in the winter. What did they think? Some people thought that swallows spent the winter underground. Other people thought they spent it underwater—beneath the ice of ponds or lakes!

### Following the Trail

See for yourself how far animals travel without getting lost. Lay a piece of tracing paper over a world map. Draw the migration routes of the arctic tern, the monarch butterfly, and the loggerhead sea turtle. Use a different color pencil or marker for each animal.

Now that you know how to find your way, you're ready to go out and explore. And here are some other books and some web sites you might enjoy exploring, too!

## Books

*Far Out!*
*A Guide to Exploring Nature with Binoculars*
By Christina Wilsdòn

*The Sierra Club Wayfinding Book*
By Vicki McVey

*Mapping the World*
By Sylvia A. Johnson

*Where Am I?*
*The Story of Maps and Navigation*
By A. G. Smith

*Maps*
*Getting from Here to There*
By Harvey Weiss

*The Reader's Digest Children's*
*Atlas of the World*

## Web Sites

www.readersdigestkids.com
Find out about other great Reader's Digest children's books. Look for Pathfinders, On the Spot Books, and Windows on Science.

www.nationalgeographic.com/kids
Visit "Xpeditions" and click on "Atlas" for maps you can print out and color. Test your knowledge of geography with "GeoBee Challenge."

www.afterschool.gov
Check out this web site for links to lots of United States government web sites for kids.

www.eduweb.com
You'll find adventures in history and geography on this web site.

# Glossary

**altitude:** The vertical distance or height of a celestial body (such as a star) above the horizon.

**astronomer:** A scientist who studies the universe.

**axis:** An imaginary line that stretches from the North Pole through the center of Earth to the South Pole. Earth rotates around its axis.

**bearing:** Direction measured from one place to another using a compass.

**cardinal points:** North, south, east, and west.

**celestial navigation:** Using the sun and stars to figure out direction.

**compass:** A tool with a freely moving magnetized needle that always points to magnetic north.

**constellation:** A group of stars that forms a pattern in the sky.

**core:** The central, or innermost, section of an object.

**current:** The regular flow of liquid in a certain direction.

**destination:** The place where a journey ends.

**geographical north:** True north, or the point where Earth's axis passes through the North Pole.

**GPS (Global Positioning System):** A system of satellites, radio signals, and receivers used to tell where you are and how to get where you are going.

**gyrocompass:** A compass that points to true north and is not affected by Earth's magnetism.

**imprinting:** The way some young animals learn behavior from a parent or parents.

**landmark:** An object in the landscape that stands out and can be used to help you find your way.

**latitude:** The distance measured in degrees north or south from Earth's equator. On a map, latitude is shown by horizontal parallel lines.

**magnet:** An object that attracts iron- or steel-bearing objects.

**magnetic field:** The area of magnetic forces surrounding a magnet (or Earth).

**magnetic north:** A compass needle points in this direction.

**magnetite:** A mineral with magnetic properties.

**map:** A flat chart or diagram of an area.

**migrate:** To move from one place to another.

**naturalist:** A person who studies nature.

**navigate:** To find one's way.

**orbit:** The path of one object around another object. Earth orbits the sun. The moon orbits Earth.

**orient:** To line up a map in relation to a compass and landmarks you can see.

**poles:** Two opposite points. Earth's axis passes through the North Pole and the South Pole.

**satellite:** An object that orbits a larger object. The moon is a natural satellite. A GPS satellite is an artificial, or manmade, satellite.

**scale:** A measure that shows how the distance between places on a map relates to the real distance.

**symbol:** Something that stands for something else.

**ultralight airplane:** A lightweight aircraft that usually carries one person.

# Index

*Afoot and light-hearted I take to the open road,*
*Healthy, free, the world before me,*
*The long brown path before me leading wherever I choose.*

—*Walt Whitman*